sundance
publishing

LITTLE RED
READERS

Brutus Learns to Fetch

PETER SLOAN &
SHERYL SLOAN

Illustrated by Pat Reynolds

One day we taught
our dog, Brutus, to fetch.
From then on, he loved
to bring things to us.
The things belonged
to other people.

On Monday, he fetched
a neighbor's newspaper.
"Do not fetch newspapers,"
we told Brutus.
We had to return
the newspaper.

On Tuesday, he fetched
a shirt from a clothesline.
"Do not fetch shirts,"
we told Brutus.
We had to return the shirt.

4

On Wednesday, he fetched
our friend's kitten.
"Do not fetch kittens,"
we told Brutus.
We had to return the kitten.

On Thursday, he fetched
a hose from a garden.
"Do not fetch hoses,"
we told Brutus.
We had to return the hose.

On Friday, he fetched
a teddy bear from a stroller.
"Do not fetch teddy bears,"
we told Brutus.
We had to return
the teddy bear.

On Saturday, Brutus fetched
Dad's lost car keys.
"You can fetch lost keys,"
we told Brutus.
Now he fetches only keys.